STIR OUR SOUR SPIRITS

Eutha Scholl

PROFESSIONAL PUBLISHING MEETS POWERFUL PROMOTION

A wholly owned subsidiary of TBN

Stir Our Spirits
Trilogy Christian Publishers
A Wholly Owned Subsidiary of Trinity Broadcasting
Network
2442 Michelle Drive
Tustin, CA 92780

Library of Congress Cataloging-in-Publication Data is
available.
ISBN: 978-1-68556-845-0
ISBN: 978-1-68556-846-7

Contents

Foreword

With the turn of EVERY page of this book, I found myself reflecting on my own personal journey in life. I have known Eutha Scholl for close to forty years and as a personal friend and neighbor; we have shared in the mountain top and valley depths that life can bring. We share in the blessings of sons just weeks apart in age and a few years later the sorrow of losing my home and everything in the Cedar Firestorm of 2003.

In the most recent book of Eutha's, she knits the importance of faith and an eternal perspective with these experiences of life. I have often referred to quotes as a vitamin of thought for the mind. In this book, the poetry, journal reflections, and biblical references are nourishment for the soul. I have faithfully kept a journal for over forty-five years and many times through writing I untangle my thoughts through the tip of my pen. Eutha has helped me to untangle some of my thoughts and emotions through her writing. May you allow this book to offer comfort, strength, and laughter as you read and walk with Eutha through this journey of life.

By Thomas Frederick Bolz, retired elementary school teacher from Kingsway Academy and Cajon Valley Union School District, Assistant Pastor with Emmanuel Christian Church, and Radio Commentator on GodRadio1.com.

Dedication

I dedicate this book to my cousin Jamie, who is very passionate about life, yet still finds time, to slow down and listen to the stirrings of the Spirit in her life. You've inspired me to step out of myself and follow the stirrings of God in my heart.

Preface

The gentle breeze of the Spirit that stirs the leaves, the gifts in our life's which then respond to God's calling on our lives, can easily be turned by Satan, into a place of chaos, it can become a mighty raging wind, scattering us to the winds of fear and anxiety, causing us to move away from the stirrings of the Spirit in our lives, leaving us feeling scattered, worn and tired. We need to guard our heart, and mind in Christ Jesus, Phillipines 4:7, AMP, "And that peace which reassures the heart, that peace, which transcends all understanding, that peace which stands guard over our hearts and minds in Christ Jesus, will be yours. It becomes peace "A quiet heart within."

Blessings Eutha

Other books by Eutha

Secret Places of the Heart.

Quiet Reflections

Teachings on the Heart of the Father

Stir our Spirits

Our Spirit Stirs

Oh Lord, God, of heaven and earth, stir up our spirits as You did in the house of Judea in Ezra 1:5 stirring them to rebuild Your Temple in Jerusalem. Stir up our spirits to seek Your face, stir our hearts to seek Your word, to walk in Your ways. So that we may do what You have called us to do in love and humbleness, remembering that our success comes from Your Spirit within us. Stir our hearts to know Your voice, because we also know the evil one would stir our hearts, causing us to focus on earthly things, keeping our spirits in turmoil, in strife, anger, jealousy, drawing us away from Your stirrings in our heart. Where do you find yourself, whose voice is stirring your spirit? God's Spirit within you? Or the voice of the world pulling you away from your Father. When God's Voice stirs your spirit, to do something, to move outward in ministry to others, you will face opposition from the enemy of your soul, seeking to pull you into worldly passions and lies. Seek your Father's voice, listen carefully to whatever He has stirred your heart to do. You can trust Him to strengthen you and His Spirit to encourage you, as you listen to His stirrings deep within your soul.

Footprints of the Heart

As we walk through the Footprints of Your word, you leave Your footprints on our hearts, showing us the way home. Yet Lord, sometimes Your footprints seem obscured, washed away by the storms of life. I look back, and I see one set of footprints, that's when I live by faith, knowing You carried me through the storm. In the book of Hebrews 13:5 You tell us, "Never will I forsake you, never under any circumstances will I leave you without support." When the storms of life give you fear, look ahead as the storms disappear, letting the sun shine through, you will once again see two sets of footprints in the sand as he now walks beside you on your journey of faith.

The Morning Star

As I awaken, He chases away the shadows of my dreams. As Christ the morning star arises within me, I sense His footprints upon my heart, as I arise to this new day. I worship Him, in a spirit of reverence and adoration. Come people come, worship Him with me, in the splendor of his Holiness. Let Him clear away the dark cobwebs of yesterday in your heart. On that day of darkness on the cross, living waters flow down through time. So far away from the glory of His father, He felt the pain of separation. As darkness surrounded him, Satan and his demons laughed in the face of God. As He lay in the tomb of darkness, the angels wept. Three days later, a light began to shine in the tomb. Awakening Him with power. The stone could not hold Him. The soldiers, the demons fled in fear, as He walked out of that tomb of darkness as the Lion of Judea. With the power of His father upon him, He roared "Let my people go! I paid the price. I am the final sacrifice." Let us praise Him as David did in his Psalms 16:8, "Oh give thanks to the Lord. Call upon His name." Make know His deed among the people. Sing praises of worship, sing glory to His name.

The Cross

The darkness is full of shadows, as I awaken before the dawn, even the rooster is still slumbering. I sit here in the early light worshipping You. Knowing that You who created night, also created the dawn. I come before You in the shadow of the cross. Where darkness and light clashed almost 2,000 years ago, vying for the souls, of the sons of earth. You battled with Your very life, becoming the final sacrifice. Open my spiritual eyes to see and understand, (adapted from Mathew 26:53) where he tells us, that 12 legions of angels awaited the spoken word from the Father, so that they could avenge, God's Son their Lord. You could have called down the very forces of light, instead with Your last breath You whispered, Luke 23:34, "Father forgive them, they know not what they do."

This early morning, where do you find yourself? Which side of the cross do you believe? Was Jesus just a man, battling for his life? Or was He the Son of God? Battling for the souls of man? The answer will decide where you spend eternity. Proverbs 3:10, "He has put eternity in the heart of man."

The Cross Beam of Life

Do you ever think about the cross? The cross beam, that Jesus carried up the Via Dela Rosa that day 2,000 years ago, the very weight of it, on His whipped mangled shoulders. Do you ever ask yourself, *why*? Why did He endure the weight, the pain?

Let's come closer to home. Do you ever feel like the weight of the world is on your shoulders? Pressing you into the ground? Your very spirit is weighed down with life.

Jesus took your weight that day, upon Himself, He carried it to the cross, where He permanently engraved you on the palms of His hands through the nail scars of the soldiers. Isaiah 49:16, "Behold I have engraved you on the palms of My hands;" He carried the weight of your sins, your burdens, the weight of things pressing you down, He nailed them to the cross. The cross made a shadow that day long ago on the ground, that reverberated into the heavenlies, drawing a line between darkness and light. Opening the door into the spirit world unto the great throne of God. John 14:6, "Jesus said to him, I am the way the truth and the light. No one comes to the Father except through me."

Where do you find yourself this day? Are you tired and weary? Is life too much to bear, are the ghosts of the past anger, jealousy, unforgiveness, bitterness toward life, catching up with your todays? Take them to the foot of the cross, you don't have to go far, just within your heart resides your Savior, saying to you, Mathew 11:28-29 "Come to me, all you who are weary and heavily burdened, and I will give you rest, take My yoke upon you, and learn from Me, for I am gentle and lowly in heart, there you will find rest for your soul."

Samuel

In 1ˢᵗ Samuel 3:3, we find the oil in the lamp of the Lord had not yet gone out, where young Samuel was sleeping in the temple of the Lord, where the ark of God was kept. The word of the Lord was rare in those days. Samuel did not yet know the voice of the Lord. The Lord called to Samuel, Samuel! Samuel! "Samuel went to Eli the priest, saying 'Here I am you for called me.' Two times the Lord called young Samuel in this manner, Samuel thought Eli had called him, for he had no personal experience with the voice of the Lord, Then Eli understood it was the Lord calling to the boy. Eli said to Samuel, 'Go lie down, and if He calls again, you shall say, Speak lord for your servant is listening' So Samuel went and laid down in his place. The Lord came and stood and called as at the previous times, 'Samuel! Samuel!' Then Samuel answered 'Speak Lord for your servant listens.'"

When God calls to you, where will he find you? Or like young Samuel, would you even recognize His voice? Would He find you in the quiet listening for His voice? Do you find yourself in a constant state of hurry, frustrated and maybe even angry, feeling the pressures of the day? The day is over, yet you still feel the pressures of the world around you. It's as if nothing went right. You cry out, "Where are you God?" Ask yourself, *can God speak over the noise of your life, or over the cries of your complaints to Him*? He longs to calm your cries, as a mother to a newborn baby, Psalms 116:2 tells us, "He bends down to listen." Then as you quiet your spirit before Him, He begins to whisper words of love and comfort.

Yes, God can shout over the noise of your life, but would you hear Him? He prefers to whisper to your soul, in the quiet times. Several times in His word we read where Jesus slipped away into the night and prayed. If Jesus needed quiet time with the Father how much more do we need to spend time lingering before Him? Remember as you lay out our heart before Him in prayer, He bends down and listens Psalms 116:1-2 "I love the lord, because He hears my pleas, my cries, my needs. Because He has inclined His ear to me, I will call upon him as long as I live.

Burning Bush

In Exodus 3:3-4, We find Moses standing in the desert before a burning a bush. Moses said, "I will turn aside to see this great sight, why this bush is not burned." When the Lord saw that Moses turned aside to see, God called to him out of the burning bush, "Moses! Moses!" and Moses answered, "Here I am"

This a very interesting verse, in our lives, are we so busy with our plans, that we miss the burning bush in front of us, the very voice of God. Do we in unusual circumstances, turn aside, or even stop to see? God waits for us in the most unexpected places. What an awesome thing that the God who created us, waits for us to listen. We must stop and consider Proverbs 16:9, "A man's mind plans his ways, as he journeys through life. But the Lord directs his steps." Is there a burning bush in your life, someplace where God wants to meet you? Yet you fail to turn aside and listen. My heart is saying, "Where are you Lord, how do I find your burning bush? Are you waiting in, not a physical place, like you did with Moses, or are you found deep inside our heart? Where the power of God is so strong, that we feel led in one direction or another, causing us to turn aside into our destiny? Where we rise up and say, "Here I am." Do we speak from our heart, like young Samuel did in 1st Samuel, "Speak lord for your servant listens" Isaiah 30:21, "And your ears shall a word behind you, "This is the way, walk in it." whenever you turn to the right or to the left."

We may not end up where we thought we were going, but we always end up, where we are meant to be.

Breathe of God

Once again, I find myself seeking You. I search the rising of the winds where the eagles fly. I go into the deepest sea searching for Your presence. My heart yearns within me as I seek Your face. I cry out, "Abba Father, where are You?" I begin to cry as a child who needs her father. Then I sense Your comforting voice deep within me. "Be still, my child, I am but a breath away. I created you. I breathed into you your life." "There is life in the breath of God." Man did not come alive until God breathed into him life. In John 20:22 "Jesus breathed on them and said receive the Holy Spirit." Wow! First God Himself breathed life into our physical bodies, then "Jesus breathed upon them and gave us Spiritual life." The very breathe of His Spirit is in you. You cannot physically see Him, but He is there, dwelling within you. You must tell others, come and see I have found Him the king of the Jews. Jesus Christ, our Lord. He who dwells within us, in the deep recesses of our heart. You know Him because He the Holy Spirit, lives in you continually. What do you find yourself believing? Do you sense His presence? Does He live in you guiding and directing your day? Does your spirit reflect back to those around you that the king of the Jews resides in your heart? Can you say with certainty, "Come and see, I found have found Him the King of the Jews?

Walking through the Valley

Heartbreak happens to all of us, it can come in waves, and wash over us like a heavy rain at times most surprising. Loss begins to feel like a physical loss, an emptiness that can't be explained or put into words. Mending a broken heart, can seem monumental, and at times impossible. People tell us "You will get over it.' The cliché is "Time heals all wounds" The truth is, we don't get over it, it doesn't magically go away, the pain, the feeling of loss that we feel, letting us know we are walking through the valley of the shadow of death. The valley of deep darkness that surrounds our pain. So, what do we do, how do we move on? We ask, "Where are You God, in all this darkness I can't find You?" Yet Psalms 23 tells us that "The Lord is my shepherd" verse 4 "Even though I walk through the valley of the shadow of death, I will fear no evil for Thou art with me. Your rod and Your staff they comfort me." The darkness, the pain surrounds us, but Jesus walks beside us, slowly bringing us into the light, speaking softly to our spirit, whispers of love, He understands the loss, He understands the pain, He was separated from His father on the cross "My God, my God why have You forsaken me?" He was from His very heart crying out, "Father why have You left me?" Jeremiah 23:23 "We do not have a God who is faraway, but a God who is near." His word tells us in Psalms 147:3, "He heals the brokenhearted and binds up their wounds" Give Him your pain, give Him your feeling of loss, cry out before Him, let Him slowly walk with you through the valley, till you reach the Son light on the other side, where your loved ones are waiting for you.

The Lion of Judea

Genesis 49:8-10 tells us the lion is the symbol of the tribe of Judah. Revelation 5:5 tells us that Jesus came from the tribe of Judah, "Look closely, the Lion of the tribe of Judah the root of David, has overcome, and has conquered!"

Lions symbolize power, fierceness, and majesty. Lions are known as the king of the beast. Jesus is known as the King of the universe. He is not afraid of his enemies; He protects His people through his death and resurrection. The lion of Judah comes in all power and majesty. Praise the lord, all His people, The Lion is aroused from His lair, He comes in all majesty and power, from above He comes. Let the watchmen sound the trumpet on the wall. "Arise, oh people let us go up to Zion, to the Lord our God." It is better to accept His power and majesty, then to deny His Kingship, and experience His wrath.

Mighty Lion

Hear the mighty lion roar, as the Lion of Judah rises from His throne. See the Lion of Judah that death could not hold. The Lion of Judah, the Son of God comes to war with the one who deceives His people. The one who would sit on the throne of our hearts, deceiving us with false promises. Hear the Lion roar, "Let my people go" as He stands in front of the tomb, where death could not hold Him. "Let my people go, I paid the price." Blessings, honor, glory, wisdom, thanksgiving, power and might be to God forever and ever. Revelation 5:5, "One of the elders said to me, weep no longer, behold the Lion of Judah, the root of David has conquered."

Jeremiah 25:30, "The Lord will roar from on high, and utter his voice from His holy dwelling;"

Amos 3:8, "The Lion has roared! Who will not fear? The Lord has spoken. Who can but prophesy?"

Hear The Mighty Roar

Oh Lord, oh Lord, how majestic is Your name in all the earth. See the eagle in flight, who speaks of the majesty of Your creation, who flies toward the very veil of heaven, as he circles the earth. Bold and beautiful is the lion, hear him roar, as he steps from his lair, announcing the dawn of a new day. As we listen to the hyena laugh, we hear You laugh in derision at Your enemies. Oh Lord, oh Lord, how majestic is Your name in all the earth.

See the majesty of the eagle, hear the roar of the lion, open your ears, as you hear the laugh of the hyena. You will find God's voice, in the roar of the ocean, in the wind in the trees, you'll hear His majesty. Psalms 65:8 tells us, "You make the dawn and the sunset shout for joy." You need not look far to hear his voice, sometimes He's just a whisper in your heart.

"Oh Lord, oh Lord, how majestic is Your name in all the earth."

Dusty Roads

As I walk through the dry dusty roads of life, I sense darkness pressing in on every side, I seek your face, as I turn my face toward heaven I pray for wisdom, wisdom to navigate my way home, wisdom to turn my face, to look upon Your holiness, while I'm hemmed in, in darkness on every side. I find my courage to walk forward in you. Adapted from Proverbs 2:20, "I will walk in the way of good men and keep to the path of the righteous," My heart will not be weighed down by evil, but will be lifted up by your Spirit, soaring in joy to the very edge of heaven, The dry dusty road no longer makes me feel alone, for my spirit senses your Spirit walking beside me. "Haley DiMarco" We may know our destination, but it is in the day- by- day living, the journey, that is the journey that strengthens our faith ." Faith that knows just because the thunder clouds of darkness roar, the Lion of Judea roars even louder, calling us home. 2 Thessalonians 3:3 tells us, "But the Lord is faithful, He will establish you, and guard and protect you from the evil one." Look up, oh His people for your Redeemer drawth nigh!

Abiding

One of the most essential elements for us spiritually, is to have an abiding relationship with the Father, getting to know the Father's heart. We need to linger in His presence. Webster's defines the word linger, "As lasting for a long time or slow to end." Those who develop an intimate relationship with the Father, on a daily basis, will be equipped to sustain life's greatest storms. In Exodus 33:11 we read, "When Moses returned to the camp, Joshua the son of Nun, Moses, aid, would not depart from the tent, he lingered before the lord." Whither the storms around you originate from hell's fury, or the worlds distractions, so many things can pull us away from spending time with the Father. Psalms 46:10 reminds us, "Be still and know that I am God" "I will be exalted among the nations." "I will be exalted in the earth." We exalt Him when we spend time with Him, lingering, abiding and worshiping Him, listening to His heart.

I believe that God chose Joshua to lead the people after Moses, because God knew Joshua's heart. Because as we read in Exodus 33:11, "Joshua had spent time lingering before the Lord." What powers our public ministry is the time we spend in intimate fellowship with the Father.

Eagles Wings

As a mother eagle flies under her young, to catch them as they learn to fly so that they may settle on her back or wings if necessary, so to Your Spirit flies under us to catch us if we fall. Psalms 91:4, "He will cover you and completely protect you under His pinions, under His wings you will find refuge." We get anxious as we see darkness on the horizon, we rise up on eagle's wings, above the storms of life, to enter into Your presence. You hide us there, on eagle's wings. You speak to our hearts in this season of darkness, In Exodus 19:4 You tell us, "You have seen what I did to the Egyptians, and how I carried you on eagle's wings and bought you to Myself.' To make Isaiah 40:31 speak to our heart's let's personalize it. "You will lift up your wings and rise up close to God, rising toward the sun, you will run and not become weary, you will walk and not grow tired." As we rise to meet You, Psalms 65:8 comes to mind, "You make the dawn and the sunset shout for joy" Your hollowed hands have made me, and established me. Remember always this word and promise to your servant.

Waiting Room

Sometimes, we find ourselves in the waiting room of life, whether it be the physical or the spiritual we need to prepare, through learning and life challenges, how to prepare for the step ahead. We find in the in the Old Testament that Moses spent forty years living in Egypt, learning leadership abilities, and then spent another forty years of his life living in the desert, learning the very places he would later lead the Jews through. While we wait in the waiting room of life, where sometimes it seems nothing is happening, we should spend time learning the lessons around us. It teaches us the ability to handle the future we don't yet understand, God doesn't show us the staircase, sometimes it's only the first step we must take. Keep seeking His presence, stay close as you stop and learn. Move with the cloud, as Israel did during the day while traveling in the desert. Keep pressing on. When the down times come, and they will, rest in the fire. We see Israel, Daniel, and David anointed twenty years before he actually became king. Even Paul of the New Testament, rested in the Spirit of God as they prepared for their future ministries. Bravery and courage are nothing more than pressing on and learning the lessons of life while we wait.

Warriors for Christ

Today something occurred to me. Do I have a warrior's heart, or a intercessors heart? Where do find yourself, wanting to run as David did toward the battle line to fight Goliath, or wanting to spend time lingering quietly before the father, in intersession? A warrior is fueled by the prayers of the intercessor, the intercessor is fueled by the time they spend time before the Father. In the book of Deuteronomy, we find Joshua lingering in the tent of the meeting before God. God knew his heart. He eventually became a mighty warrior leading the army of God into battle. The priest who supported Joshua was Eleazar. The Torah tells us in Numbers 27:21 That God said to Moses, "Joshua will come and go at the word of Eleazar the Priest." Eleazar supported Joshua before God. He became Joshua's counselor spiritually. Where do you find yourself, are you called to be the visible warrior, or the hidden away, special ops intercessor on your knees going in before the Lord, making a way for the warriors to do battle through your prayers? Both warriors and intercessors are part of God's army, just because you're not visible, doesn't mean you are not needed. Just as Joshua was accountable to Eleazar the Priest, we each in our lives must be accountable to someone, to mentor us, to guide us in the ways of the lord.

Cisterns of Sand

Sometimes, we have heart wounds, that weigh us down. Keeping us down, in a dry sandy cistern, a well of darkness. The dryness of a heart filled with wounds of anger, unforgiveness. Come Holy Spirit and fill this well with your springs of living water. Overflowing into our lives, cleansing our wounds, with the living water of your Spirit. Raising us up from the cistern of darkness, so that those who stumble, who live in darkness, who thirst after spiritual things, may sense the springs of living water in us. Revelation 22:17, "Let the one who is thirsty come; let the one who desires take the water of life without price." Holy Spirit stir our spirits that we may reach up out of the dryness of life and into your springs of living water.

Appearance of the Heart

1ˢᵗ Samuel 16:7, "For the Lord sees not as man sees; for man looks at the outward appearance, but the Lord looks at the heart."

The question that comes to mind is, does God look upon the inner man because that's where our hidden gods are, the god's we think no one else see's? Gods of the flesh. Do we desire things of the flesh instead of things of the Spirit.? Do we seek our hidden gods, that we try to hide, even from God? Money, fame, even in religious circles, seeking wisdom for our personal gain. Have we become like the pharisees, whitewashed tombs seeking out other religious people? Remember, God looks deep into the heart. God want to get to very heart of the matter. Our Christian walk, our relationship with God must start from the inside out. Giving up to the Spirit our God's of pride, and humanity, gods of self. Ask yourself, where do I find myself this morning? Reaching out first to the world of social media, our computer, our cells phones, or do we find ourselves seeking the Spirit? Do we seek a quiet place, away from the white noise of life, humanity? Do find ourselves in the quiet of the morning saying," Speak lord for your servant listens?"

God tells us in Job 33:33, "Listen to Me, and be silent, I will grant you wisdom."

When Father, When?

The day stretches out before us like the ocean, reflecting the morning sun. Stretching to the farthest horizons. Connecting Your people of all races, color and creed. I see children, teenagers, adults, young and old. You see the many hearts crying out to You. The many hands in worship. The many voices, in many countries crying out to You, we ask, "When Father when, when will this final battle between good and evil be done?" When Father when, will You return to take us home?" We are weary, Your people Lord. We await Your return, to take us to a place of peace, a place of no sickness, of no war. A place of joy. A place where evil is not known. The question we need to ask is "Do we cower in fear as we wait, or do we march forward as warrior brides, of our King?"

Ezra 8:23, "So we fasted and prayed concerning this matter, and He heard our plea."

Psalms 116:2, "Because He bends down to listen, I will pray as long as I have breathe!"

Seeking God

In Genesis 3:10 Adam said, "I heard the sound of you walking in the garden, and was afraid because I was naked; so, I hid myself." The question is why are we even today, afraid of God? We don't seek Him for ourselves. We seek others about His word. As the Israelites told Moses in the desert, do we find ourselves also saying, "You seek the Lord for us, then come tell us what He is saying," In fear we tremble before Him.

Do we rely on the Prophets, the Pastors, the Teachers, to search out the word of God then come tell us what He is saying to us? Jesus died so that we could have a relationship with the Father, so we could hear for ourselves His words to us, no longer do we need someone to intercede for us. Jesus alone intercedes for us. When the temple veil tore in two when Jesus died, it opened a spiritual veil between heaven and earth, granting us access to the Father. Like He had with Adam, God desires a relationship with us. To walk with us in the cool of the evening. Are we afraid of God? Do we feel like we're naked before Him? That he would see the darkness, the confusion in our hearts? Do we feel unworthy? The very God who created us, longs to love His creation. Yet we keep Him at arm's length. When He speaks in our heart, "Come abide with Me" We send someone else in our place to tell us what He has to say. Jeremiah 6:10, "Their ears are closed so they cannot hear." What are we afraid of? Why do we run from seminar to seminar, seeking to be inspired by what others say, when He is within us, His Holy Spirit dwells in us speaking to our hearts? 1 Corinthians 6:19, "Do you not know that your body is a temple of the Holy Spirit within you, whom you have from God?"

Old Roads

1 Samuel 8:5-8, "When Samuel became old, he made his son's Judges over Israel. Yet his sons did not walk in his ways, but turned aside after gain, they took bribes and perverted justice. They did not walk in the ways of their father, they made their own rules, not according to what their father lived and believed." The Jews begin to cry out because of the chaos, to go back to the old ways. You tell us in your word, Isaiah 46:9, "Remember the former things of old, for I am God there is no other, I am God there is no one like me." Find where the good is; then walk in it, you will find rest for your souls." But Samuel's sons said," We will not walk in it!" Jeremiah 18:12, "But they will say, we are going to follow our own plans, each of us will walk in accordance with stubbornness of his evil heart."

Today's culture is trying so hard to forget our past. To erase history as we know it. I don't understand, except without our history, the roads, the precepts of the past, we lose our footing. Our way of life as we understand, and know it, becomes obsolete. The new culture wants to throw off, as they see it, old ways, old rules, old morality, they cry, "we will create things our way, no rules, except what we want them to be." New morality says, be whoever, or what every you want to be, as long as it feels good. They chant, "We want our freedom." The problem becomes, freedom without authority is not freedom, it turns into chaos! Who do we let make the new rules? How do we go back to the old ways, the ways of God? "Samuel!" the Jews cried out of the chaos, "Grant us a king to judge us." The Lord said to Samuel, "Obey the voice of the people. For they have not rejected you, they have rejected me from being king over them." He also told Samuel to tell the people, "And in that day you will cry out because of your king that you have chosen for yourself, but the lord will not answer you in that day."

Psalms 119:52 :62, "When I think of your rules from of old, I take comfort Lord." At midnight I rise up to praise you, because of your righteous rules.

Christ Like

I believe that in the greatness of the need, there are more opportunities to show forth the love of God. To show forth His hands reaching down into hurting people's lives. I personally believe that each and every one of us who calls ourselves a Christian, is to be Christ like, to be God with skin on. To do the things we find within our hand, and on a daily basis demonstrate the hands of God's love reaching into people's lives. So that they may look at and see the very person of Jesus, looking through our eyes. Jeremiah 23:3, "We have a God who is near and not far away."

"When the suffering is the greatest, the harvest will be most plentiful." Adapted from James Murphy

Shiloh

The word stress was originally an engineering term used to refer to the amount of force that a beam or other physical support could bear without collapsing under the strain. In our time, stress has expanded to include mental, or emotional tension, (Joyce Meyer)

We need to remember, that Christ's peace operates in the very middle of life's storms. When the emotional or mental tension is at its worst, He gives us His peace when we chose, to listen and obey. Micah 5:5, "This one, the Messiah shall be our peace.' When you are feeling stressed, when life seems to have turned upside down, go down to Shiloh, that place in your soul where the living waters flow. Isaiah 8:4, "Then he will become a sanctuary, a sacred place, a shelter for those who fear and trust him."

Where do you find yourself as you read this, torn, weary, does the term "a quiet heart" seem far from your reach? "We need to learn and understand the things that causes us to lose our peace." We need to shut out the noise of life, and spend time with the Father, asking Him to show us the things that cause our peace to flee. Sometimes, the very things that we think we control, are what's causing our peace to flee. Give control of your life, your relationships, your work. Even your spiritual life can be stressful if we serve God in a works related relationship. Philippians 4:7, "And the peace of God which Transcends all understanding, that peace which guards your heart and mind, in Christ Jesus will be yours."

In Times Like These

Whispers of angel wings awaken me. As the night turns into day, I welcome them. They whisper as the Son of the morning star comes galloping on His white stead, asking me to join in the battle just a breath away. The final battle has begun, with the sound of the shofar, He calls his people out of slumber into battle. He whispers to my heart, Isaiah 48:8, "Do not tremble, nor be afraid of the violent upheavals to come. Do not be afraid of events that are going to take place." Listen now with an open ear. The angel wings flutter around us like doves calling into the night as they cry, holy, holy, holy, is He who sits on the throne. Isaiah 33:22, "For the Lord is our judge, the Lord is our ruler, the Lord is our king; He will save us." "Listen carefully, as the angels hold their breath, I am about to do a new thing, even now it springs forth." Isaiah 13:4, "A sound of tumult on the mountains, like that of many people! A sound of uproar of the kingdoms. Of nations gathered together! The Lord of hosts is mustering an army for battle. They are coming from a distant country. The Lord and the weapons of His indignation." Adapted from Isaiah 43:21, "As the people who I formed for myself will make my praises known, I, only I, am the Lord, there is no Savior besides Me." Acts :13:41, "For I am doing a work in your days, a work which you will never believe, even if someone describes it to you in detail."

Gateway to My Soul

You guard with your Holy Spirit the very life that is within me. At the gateway to my soul, You stand. Where heaven meets earth deep within me, is where You stand. It is there where the battle forms its deepest fight. Where light and darkness battle for my soul. At the gateway to eternity is where You stand. Guarding the gateway to my soul.

Holy Spirit, I open the door to receive you. Come live, there deep within in the recesses of my soul. The fight is not mine but Yours. I am weak yet You are strong. To meet the enemy at the gateway of my soul is Your desire. The door to heaven is found there deep within.

We ask ourselves where is the gateway, that leads to our soul? The Spiritual gateway includes our five senses, the eyes, what do find yourself viewing, the ears, what do you let into your heart through your ears? The mouth, what is in our heart becomes our spoken word. Touch, to touch a baby, to touch someone grieving, to give hope through our touch, is not the same as the sensual touch of an unknown person we've let into our life. Our senses need to be controlled by the Spirit within us. Do we use our spiritual senses to glorify God, or to seek the ways of the world?

Sleeping with the Enemy

Satan often attacks us from within, infiltrating our closest relationships. Sometimes those closest to us, are the enemy dressed in disguise. Yet because we can't see beyond the physical, we need the discernment of the Spirit, because sometimes the enemy looks, walks, and talks just like us. Be careful who you align yourself with, even Jesus had Judas. The enemy of our soul may come to take our physical freedom, even our very life, but he can never take the freedom inside our soul, true freedom lies within us. Galatians 5:1, "It was for this freedom Christ has set us free." 2 Corinthians 3:17, "Now the Lord is the Spirit, where the Spirit of the Lord is there is freedom." 1 Corinthians 3:16, "Do you not know you are God's temple? God's Spirit dwells within you. God's temple is holy. you are that the temple. If anyone destroys God's temple God will destroy him." We yearn for peace, but sometimes we only find it through spiritual warfare. Stand firm therefore and see the salvation of the Lord. His death on the cross has set us free.

Early Dawn

Early will I seek Thee, in the dawn of the new day I will come before You, as the sun arises over the mountain top's I bring my offering of praise. Psalms 65:8, "The whole earth is filled with awe at Your wonders, where morning dawns, where evening fades. You call forth songs of joy." In Psalms 8:17 we read, "I love those who love me, and those who seek me early and diligently, will find me."

Where do you find yourself this morning? Tired, weary of life, dreading the new day? Staring into your coffee wondering what this day will bring? Come outside, see the sun arise on the dawn of this new day, meet your creator, the one who breathed into you the very breath of life. The one who makes the dawn and the sunset shout for joy, Psalms 71:7, "I am as a wonder to many, for you are my strong refuge, my mouth is filled with your praise and your glory all the day long." Joyce Meyers reminds us that, "Joy comes from a decision to appreciate each moment you are given as a rare and precious gift from God." Come, the Son arises.

Sacrifice of Praise

In the Hebrew language, the word sacrifice, is translated "Zabuck" literally meaning to draw close. Rabbi Solomon Hirish, "Tells us that "Zabuck is a driving force for us, to bring a sacrifice offering to God, to bring us closer to Him."

Sacrifice, also a derivative in Greek, is pronounced "Quararn" meaning "to approach, to give up something valuable to draw close to another."

Romans 11:2, "Therefore I appeal to you brothers in view of Elohim's compassion, offer up your bodies as a living sacrifice, do not be conformed to this age, but be transformed by the renewing of your mind." Then you will be able to draw close, to offer up a sacrifice of praise.

Yes, we sacrifice to serve God in the physical sense, paying tithes and offerings, feeding the poor, sacrificing our self for the good of other's. It's not about what we do, it's not about the promise of money, or because of what He can give us. It's first and foremost about drawing close, praising, and worshiping the God who created us. All things flow from that.

A sacrifice of praise is when we approach God through Jesus, with a longing and a hunger, to draw close, to be near Him, with the thought that our love and praise are enough for Him. It's not about what we do, it's about our relationship with Him. All things flow from that. The greatest offering, we can give is of ourselves, body, soul, and spirit.

Buttons

We've all had our buttons, our emotional reactions, pushed at some time or another, to the point we can't take it anymore. Feelings of anger flare, we say, "it's always the other person." It could be when we're crying before the Lord, we need to pray, "Lord, change me, my emotional reaction, rather than Lord change them." The more we take responsibility for our feelings and reactions, the less tender the emotional buttons become. We do however need to discern what belongs to us, and what belongs to other people. Galatians 6:5, "For every person has to bear his own faults, and shortcomings, for which he alone is responsible." We need to refuse to serve as a target for other people's anger. We are well within our rights to set boundaries with that person, be it family, friends, or co-workers. Yet underneath the pain we need to own our feelings, there's always some pain that needs to be acknowledged in order for us to heal. The one who needs attention could be us. God feels our pain but does not indulge our self- pity. Jeremiah 17:9, "I the Lord search the heart and test the mind." Freedom will finally come when we deal with the pain behind the buttons, and disconnect our reactions, our emotional responses to the situation we find ourselves in.

The Church

Instead of focusing on the number of members in our church's, what if we focus on creating an atmosphere to receive the Spirit of God, to receive His anointing, in our lives? After all isn't that what it's all about? First receiving the Spirit of God, then turning to those behind us, who are in darkness, offering them His Spirit that lives within us? The church, Christ's church, is not made of walls, but of hearts, hearts united in His love, hearts broken, over what breaks the very heart of God. Do you hear today, the whispers of God, calling you to go deeper, deeper into the living waters of His word? Calling you to listen with your heart, to the cries of people living in darkness. Ask yourself what kind of legacy do you want to leave behind? What kind of footprint do you want to leave on the hearts of those around you? People may not remember your words, but they will remember how you made them feel. Do they feel God's anointing on your life? Or do they feel you are just another religious person, with your list of rules, and programs made mostly to display your love of numbers?

Consider the Butterfly

In life, as we look back on our past, consider the butterfly. After it has done its metamorphosis, it doesn't turn and look back at the time spent in the darkness of the cocoon, with guilt, unforgiveness, or shame, it turns, spreads its wings, flying to new horizons. Why then do we hang on to the past? Constantly looking back, with shame, guilt, and unforgiveness, remembering the darkness of our past? Christ came to set us free from the past, the darkness that would entomb us.

2 Corinthians 5:17 tells us, "Therefore if any man be in Christ, he is a new creature, old things have passed away; behold all things are new."

So, look up to your creator, spread your wings as a new creature in Christ, and fly!

Fill This Temple

Our Spirits arise alone and empty. We cry, come Holy Spirit fill this temple. Let it overflow with Your glory. Let the windows of heaven rain down, filling this temple with Your Holy Presence. Let Your Spirit rise within us. Father, do you hear? Do you see? Is your heart broken over your people, who You created to be Your temple? People created to shine with Your light. Do You see the darkness, do You see the windows with no light? Rain down from heaven, the glory of Your presence, as you push back the darkness in this, Your temple, so that the light of Your power and majesty can shine through. Let Your Holy Spirit come into this temple. Let us worship You, as You rain down Your Spirit. Let it rain, let it rain, let it rain. Let Your Holy Spirit speak into the depths of our soul, of Your love, of Your holy rain. May our praises rise up as incense, as our hearts cry out in worship before you. We soak in your Holy Presence, as we soak in the gentle rain of your Spirit. As the mist of the redwood forest, waters the roots of the giant trees, God's Spirit hovers as a gentle rain over our lives, soaking down into our spirits watering the roots of a thirsty soul.

Cracked Pots

2 Corinthians 4:7, "But we have this treasure, (Your Spirit) in jars of clay. To show that the surpassed power belongs to God and not us. We are afflicted in every way, but not crushed, perplexed but not driven to despair, persecuted but not destroyed."

The world does not begin to understand how these jars of clay contain the very Spirit, of our Father in heaven. In these hard times, let me be a light to bring others with me out of the darkness on our journey home. We in our lives, have experienced much pain. The cracks run deep, from many wounds. Hurts that that don't seem to heal. I've come to realize that these cracks all serve, if we give them to you, to shine Your light brighter to reach others, who hurt, who have experienced the same hurts and pain. Grant me words to say, deeds to do, that would lift others out of the darkness that seeks to overcome them. Let me show Your love and compassion. We read in Your word, as together we begin this journey home that in Exodus 23:20, "Behold, I am going to send an angel before you, to keep and guard you on the way and bring you to the place I have prepared."

The Story of Ruth

We find in Genesis chapter 19, that when God destroyed the valley of Sodom and Gomorrah, God remembered His servant Abraham, because of His great love for Abraham, God sent Lot, Abraham's nephew, and his family out of the city of Sodom, before the destruction came. Lot went up out of the valley with his two daughters. They lived in a cave in the mountains, his oldest daughter said, "Come there are no men for us, we will make our father drunk with wine, thus preserving his offspring through us. We will lie with him, thus both daughters of Lot became pregnant by him. The firstborn daughter had a son and named him Moab. (Which means Father) He became the father of the tribe of the Moabites. To this day, they are a pagan tribe worshiping many gods. Let's move down through time to the story of Ruth. Ruth was a Moabite from the nation of many gods. We read in the book of Ruth, a story of courage, a story of beauty, rising through the grace of God, from the ashes of her past. Even though she was a Moabite, she became the daughter-in-law of a Jewish woman named Naomi.

Through God's saving grace, as we read the story of her life, Ruth became the great grandmother of Jesus. Take this story and apply it to your life. As we journey through the earth, there are many gods that surround us, gods of evil, gods of self, seeking many pleasures, pride at our accomplishments, rebellion at the thought of the one true God. Gods of fame and fortune, they all pull us away from a relationship with

God the Father. When God does come into our life, He looks into our heart, the very place of our many gods. If we let Him, like Ruth, He cleanses the gods of the world away by the blood of His Son on the cross. Leaving a place to be filled, not with the gods of this world, but by his Holy Spirit. The things of the past are put away, instead of mourning the past we will rejoice in our future with Him. Isaiah 61:3, "We will be called oaks of righteousness, the planting of the lord, that he may be glorified."

Recesses of your Heart

I rise up before the break of dawn, seeking Your presence. I long within me, to be called Your friend. To walk with You in the cool of the evening while the dew falls on the roses. I whisper, "Speak Lord for your servant listens." I open my spiritual ear to hear Your voice. Your voice resounds within me. As you draw me into Your presence. I cry out with the angels, Holy, Holy, Holy is the Lord God Almighty. As you turn Your face toward heaven, I cry out "Don't leave me." You answer, "Just for a little while my friend, until my word is fulfilled. Seek My Spirit within you, I will meet you there in the deep recesses of your heart."

Have you met with Him within the dark places of your heart? Have you let the Son shine into the very places that you keep hidden from others? God sees, He desires to reach down and take your hand, to pull you up out of the deep recesses of the darkness into His light. He desires to call you friend. John 14:17, "You will know Him because He (the Holy Spirit) remains with you continually, and will be in you."

The Road Home

I seek your presence, I go into the depths of the sea, I climb the highest mountain, seeking your face, yet you are not there, my heart yearns for your presence. Then I hear a whisper, a voice so near, "I'm here within you, wherever you travel I am here, unless you choose to go alone on your journey through this dark world. Even then I am on the edge of your heart, bending down to listen. This road you will travel, is dark and cold spiritually. A great darkness is spreading, obscuring the way home. Standout, be a light post to those following you, don't blend into the darkness. As you bring my people home, teach them along the way. As you walk, as you talk, help them to see through the darkness into the future."

Luke 24:15, "While they were walking and talking together, Jesus himself drew near and went with them."

As we walk through our journey of faith, as we seek His face, He is there within us.

Psalms 116:1-2, "I love the Lord, because he has heard my plea for mercy, because he has inclined his ear to me, therefore I will call upon him as long as I live."

Ghosts of the Past

Ghosts of the past, we all have them, things in our soul that we haven't let go of. Soul ties, real or imagined, are ghosts of the past. Unforgiveness, anger, jealousies, bad relationships, all play a role of keeping us in the past. Whispers of Satan, that say we're not good enough, he haunts us with our past, always bringing to mind the things we did or said, remembering things that were done to us, abuse that damaged our soul. Things we're sorry for but remain unresolved. The ghosts continue to haunt us, at times they can be scary, not letting go. If we let the ghosts, they can consume us. Dragging us backward into a life of shame and bitterness, having unforgiveness of our self and others. In the Greek language, the definition of soul is as in Mathew 11:29 where it speaks of, "The heart, the mind, our life, our very psyche." What is the conscience theme of your soul? What is your internal dialog? In a healthy soul we listen to the forgiveness of the Father. In an unhealthy soul we listen to the whispers of Satan, "That God if he knew, won't forgive us, we hide deep inside with the ghosts of our past. Don't google your soul pain, go to God's word. There you will find love and forgiveness. A healthy soul influences the environment around them, not letting the environment influence, or change them. They go to the Father, where He will through His Spirit, protect their soul. Psalms 34:7,"The angel of the Lord encamps around those who fear him and delivers them." Satan comes to steal and destroy using the ghosts of our past, Jesus came to give life, and give it more abundantly, destroying with his words of forgiveness the ghosts of our past.

Psalms 31:1-3, "In you oh Lord do I take refuge; let me never be put to shame; In your righteousness deliver me. Incline your ear to me; deliver me quickly; Be my rock of refuge, and a strong fortress to save me."

Jobst Bittener tells us that, "The traumas that are covered by silence, are simply passed on. There is no doubt that the ghosts of the past can also be transmitted to the next generation on an emotional level."

Seasons of the Spirit

I sense Your Spirit here as this season of life draws to a close. I seek You as I journey to a new way of life in Your kingdom. As I stand on the path between heaven and earth, let me bring others with me. Others who would desire to serve You, who would desire to take this journey into Your kingdom, Joel 3:14, "Multitudes, multitudes in the valley of decision, for the day of the Lord is near." I pray that while they are in the valley they will look up and see Your hand beckoning from above. Look up oh people, look up above the storm that shakes the valley, look up, call upon Him. Jeremiah 25:30, "The Lord will roar from on high and utter His voice from His Holy dwelling;" Joel 3:17, "So you will know I am the Lord your God who dwells in Zion, My Holy Mountain." Where do you find yourself in all this change that electrifies the air? Do you look upon it in despair? Do you hear His voice above the storm? Psalms 24;17 tells us, "Wait for the Lord; be strong, let your heart take courage; wait for the Lord.' Do you hear His roar as He rises from the throne? "Let my people go I paid the price" The Mighty Lion of Judea that death could not hold.

Psalms 150:1, "Praise the Lord! "Let everything that has breath praise the Lord!"

Dance with Me

Bob Goff tells us in his book *Love Does,* love always assumes it can find a way, to express itself. God's grace works this way, it becomes a kind word, partnered with an impossible prayer, it becomes a force transmitted hand to hand in dark places. Just as in hand-to-hand combat. It reaches into dark places. Have you ever stepped outside the religious boundaries you have set around yourself? Have you reached into the darkness around you? Have you let your hand be God's hand, letting the Spirit that is within you pull people out of dark places? Are you satisfied with your religious comfort zone? Have you found yourself thinking, "We don't want those people in our church?" Do you want to move outside your comfort zone, living like Jesus, having dinner with the homeless, the prostitutes, the thieves, the non-righteous? The very people society tells us are throwaways. Pulling them up with you, teaching them to dance with you on the edge of heaven. If you don't who will?

Love vs. Warfare

We are created to worship, to worship the Holy one. Demons cannot stand against Holy Worship where there are expressions of reverence and adoration. Holy Love for our Creator. When we worship, we lose all our agendas of worldly war, we move into a Holy place. When we seek the Father's face on our knees all the clamor of earthly war ceases. We worship His Spirit within us. We begin to love people who are hurting, calling out to them "Come and see I have found Him the living water, the Messiah." We begin to seek out the lost. We in our love come up against the spirit of darkness in people. Sometimes people get so caught up in warfare they forget we are not fighting the physical person. We are fighting the demons of darkness. Ephesians 6:12, "For we battle not against flesh and blood. But against authorities against the cosmic powers of this present darkness. Against the spiritual forces of evil in the heavenly places." When we worship on the mountain top, we must bring back to the valleys the love of God. We must seek the lost, those who are bound by Satan's chains of darkness. We cannot come up against Satan's demons on our own, we must like David (with God's anointing upon him) come against them in the name of the Lord. David said to Goliath in 1 Samuel 17:4, "I come against you in the name of the lord God of Israel."

Can You Believe?

How can you say you believe, when you seek your glory from others, when you seek others' opinions around you, yet you do not seek the glory of God the Father? The only one true God. We're so quick to seek out the people we want to impress with our knowledge and expertise, that we fail to understand that God seeks people with a humble heart, a heart that says, "I can only do this because of the grace of God." In Job 33:33 God says to us, "Listen to me, be silent, and I will teach you wisdom." Our wisdom comes not from learning more theology, or from the world standards, or from the reading of many books. It comes only through the Spirit within us. 1 John 2:20, "But you have been anointed by the Holy one and you have all knowledge." 1 Peter 3:15, "But in your heart set Christ apart as Holy, acknowledging Him, giving Him first place in your life, then and only then, can we give God the glory."

Let's go Home

You came down, from Your Holy place with Your Father, You looked upon the robes of sin and shame that covered Your people in the darkness of this world and You wept. Your very heart cried out, "I must obey my Father." You exchanged Your crown of glory, for a crown of thorns upon the cross. As I drop my burdens, my sins, at Your feet, at the foot of the cross. You wash them away in the blood of Your sacrifice. I wept with joy as You put up on me robes of righteousness, dipped in the blood of the cross, so I could come home to the Father, out of the chaos of this world. I hear the roar as You stepped from the tomb as the Lion of Judea scattering the demons of darkness before You. I fell to my knees in fear and trembling. Yet in love and mercy, You picked me up and whispered to me, "I did this for you" Isaiah 49:16, "See the scars on my out stretched hands?" "Behold I have carved your image on the palms of my hands" "Step into the light, come let's go home."

CPSIA information can be obtained
at www.ICGtesting.com
Printed in the USA
LVHW020018250622
721982LV00012B/241